9/11

The Attack that Shook the World

Written by Quentin Convard
In collaboration with Etienne Lock
Translated by Rose Brichard

History 50MINUTES.com

THE 9/11 ATTACKS 1

Key information

POLITICAL AND SOCIAL CONTEXT 3

A contested election
The war on terror
The threat posed by bin Laden
The American authorities and their failures

BIOGRAPHIES 9

George W. Bush, American statesman
Osama bin Laden, Saudi-Arabian jihadist
Khalid Sheikh Mohammed, al-Qaeda Military Leader

THE 9/11 ATTACKS 15

The Twin Towers
The Pentagon
Shanksville
A humanitarian disaster

IMPACT 25

A turning point in American politics
The Patriot Act
Afghanistan and the hunt for bin Laden
Conspiracy theories

SUMMARY 32

FIND OUT MORE 35

THE 9/11 ATTACKS

KEY INFORMATION

- **When:** 11 September 2001
- **Where:** New York City, USA
- **Key figures:**
  - George W. Bush, American statesman (born 1946)
  - Osama bin Laden, Saudi-Arabian Islamist extremist (1957-2011)
  - Khalid Sheikh Mohammed, al-Qaeda military leader (born 1965)
- **Impact:**
  - The war against Afghanistan
  - The hunt for Osama bin Laden
  - The Patriot Act
- **Number of fatalities:** 2976

On 11 September 2001, the entire world was shocked to discover the news of a series of attacks on American soil. With no apparent warning on one fateful Tuesday morning, nineteen terrorists hijacked four flights and crashed them almost simultaneously into the World Trade Centre, the Pentagon and a field in Shanksville, Pennsylvania. Two hours later, the Twin Towers collapsed, bringing down with them two other nearby buildings that had not been targeted by the planes. Official figures place the death toll at 2976 victims and 19 hijackers.

This was not the first time that America was subject to an insurmountable attack by a foreign enemy. The Pearl Harbor attack by the Japanese in 1941 or the USSR's launch of Sputnik in 1957 had already seen both American hegemony and the country's image weakened in the past. However, 9/11 marked the first instance of an enemy attack on American soil. In the space of twenty minutes, the USA came hurtling into the 21st century and landed with a resounding thud.

POLITICAL AND SOCIAL CONTEXT

A CONTESTED ELECTION

The USA was attacked by al-Qaeda on 11 September 2001, just a few months after George W. Bush had entered the White House. He had emerged victorious from the election which pitted him against Democrat candidate Al Gore (born 1948), the former vice president under Bill Clinton (born 1946). The election was something of a saga, full of scandal and dramatic twists. In November 2000, the day after the vote, Bush seemed to have won the vote in Florida with the incredibly narrow majority of just 500 out of 5.9 million votes cast. Gore quickly raised concerns about various irregularities during polling, giving rise to legal and political controversy as authorities tried to establish who exactly had won; the winning candidate in Florida would be the next President of the United States.

35 days after the vote, five Supreme Court judges, appointed by George Herbert Walker Bush (born 1924) and Ronald Reagan (1911-2004), ruled in the Republican candidate's favour. Therefore, George W. Bush succeeded Bill Clinton as president thanks to 271 electoral college votes versus Al Gore's 267. The population remained calm amid this electoral chaos, however the election served to illustrate the weaknesses embedded in the American democratic system. Throughout the deliberations, the tension was palpable, not only with regards to the candidates themselves but also those close to them. When the former Texas governor arrived in the White House, it was certainly not an undisputed

victory. Furthermore, the Senate was divided between the two parties, with the Republicans having just one more senator than the Democrats. As such, Bush found himself faced with a dilemma - should he concentrate on reuniting a divided nation or instead seek to strengthen Republican dominance? In any case, he was left little time to reflect on such a question, with the shocking interruption of the 9/11 attacks becoming the key factor shaping the policies of his administration.

THE WAR ON TERROR

While the 9/11 attacks caused shock and terror due to the cruelty involved and the fact that they happened on American soil in such a spectacular manner, Islamist terrorism was not something new for the American intelligence services. In fact, it had already been one of the major talking points of the 1996 presidential election. When re-elected, Clinton announced that he would place greater emphasis on the fight against terrorism than any president before him. He did so by introducing two laws - the Antiterrorism and Effective Death Penalty Act and the Migrant's Responsibility Act. While the size of the CIA as a whole had been decreasing since 1993, the National Counterterrorism Center's staff numbers doubled, allowing them to thwart several potential attacks.

The 1990s were punctuated by numerous terrorist incidents, such as attack on the World Trade Center in 1993 and on the Khobar Towers (Saudi Arabia) which housed American soldiers in 1998. Newly emerged from the Cold War, America found itself facing the unfamiliar world of Islamism and the new powers arriving on the international political scene which could challenge its global hegemony. Pakistan and India's nuclear testing in 1998 can be viewed as a failure of international policies of non-proliferation, something of key importance to the USA. In August of the same year, the US embassies in Kenya and Tanzania were attacked, killing more than 300 people and injuring 4000 more. These terrorist tragedies echoed the 1993 attack on the World Trade Center and the attack on American military bases in Saudi Arabia in November 1995 and June 1996.

THE 1993 ATTACK ON THE WORLD TRADE CENTER

On 26 February 1993, a car bomb exploded in the World Trade Center's Tower 1 basement. Al-Qaeda - the organisation blamed for the attack - was aiming to destabilise the North Tower so it would crash into the South Tower and thus kill thousands of civilians. While the operation failed in this objective, 6 people did die and several hundred others were injured. The man at the heart of the operation was Ramzi Youssef (born 1967) who fled to Pakistan hours after the explosion. Khalid Sheikh Mohammed, who had provided funding for this bombing, was also to be a key figure in the 9/11 attacks.

Following these tragic events, the US became more and more aware that their politics and ideology were contested and being targeted by certain Islamist movements, most importantly al-Qaeda and Osama bin Laden, its mentor.

THE THREAT POSED BY BIN LADEN

While most American citizens first saw Osama bin Laden's face in the aftermath of 9/11, he was well-known to the CIA and the FBI, who had considered the millionaire as a priority target since the second half of the 1990s.

Bin Laden was known to harbour strong resentment towards the American army ever since the first Iraq war (1990-91). During the war, American troops sought to protect Saudi Arabia from Iraqi troops. While bin Laden, who had funded the Afghan revolution, was convinced that he could defeat Saddam Hussein's (1937-2006) troops, the Saudis instead turned to America for support. A delegation of American experts under the leadership of Dick Cheney (American politician, born 1941) was sent to Saudi Arabia to convince King Fahd ben Abdelaziz al-Saoud (1921-2005) to allow the USA to tackle Hussein. As such, American troops, considered as infidels by some of the population (and by bin Laden himself), swarmed the land where the Prophet Mohammed was born. Bin Laden, who was himself growing in popularity, could not ignore this affront. He first threatened the USA in 1996 when he urged Muslims to attack and damage Americans and their interests whenever possible. He reiterated this threat several more times.

Bin Laden, who was at the time living in Sudan, had therefore been under CIA surveillance since 1995. In response to threats of Saudi terrorism, American diplomats and the secret service pressured the Saudi authorities to hand over bin Laden. He was then exiled to Afghanistan which had been recently conquered by the Taliban.

Clinton therefore proceeded to order air strikes on 20 August 1998, when bin Laden arrived in Afghanistan, which was governed by Taliban extremists, due to acts of violence and their links to al-Qaeda. Clinton sought in vain to put an end to the country's troubles with bin Laden and his network with the help of the secret service and by diplomatic means. The situation did not improve and in October 2000, al-Qaeda organised an attack on the American destroyer USS Cole, anchored in Aden Port in Yemen. 17 marines were killed.

On 9 September 2001, bin Laden decided to lash out at one of his enemies, Commander Massoud (commander of the United Islamic Front for the Salvation of Afghanistan, 1953-2001), who was intent on showing the danger bin Laden represented to the international community. Two fake journalists with Belgian passports approached Massoud under the pretext that they wanted to interview him. They then set off a bomb hidden in their camera which killed Massoud. A link has now been established between this event and the 9/11 attacks.

THE AMERICAN AUTHORITIES AND THEIR FAILURES

In their fight against terrorism, the American authorities had several weaknesses.

During the Clinton administration (1993-2001), the department of the Treasury voiced opposition to an operation to strip al-Qaeda of millions of dollars, arguing that it would violate market rules. Furthermore, Clinton and Bush's advisers were convinced that China and Russia or "rogue" states who did not respect international law represented the main threats to America. This caused them to choose to ignore foreign intelligence agencies' warnings that al-Qaeda was present on American territory and ready to strike. While they knew that their bases outside the US were in considerable danger, they were overly confident with regards to the possibility of an internal threat. As such, not long before 9/11, an FBI agent's request to search a computer belonging to trainee pilot Zacarias Moussaoui (born 1968), due to his "suspect" behaviour, was denied.

BIOGRAPHIES

GEORGE W. BUSH, AMERICAN STATESMAN

George W. Bush was the 43rd president of the United States and the son of the 41st president George Herbert Walker Bush. He graduated from Yale with a history of art degree and was part of a secret elitist student society known as the Skull and Bones. He voluntarily avoided serving in the Vietnam War (1955-1975) and became part of the Colorado National Guard in 1968, where he served as a pilot. He then earned a place in the prestigious Harvard Business School and gained his MBA in 1975 before beginning a career in the oil industry. Between 1983 and 1992, he was also the director of a film production society.

DID YOU KNOW?

Skull and Bones is the name given to a secret society of elites at Yale University, created in 1830 by businessman William Huntington Russell (1908-1885). Each year, the society selects fifteen undergraduates with brilliant futures ahead as its new members. The 27th US president William Taft (1857-1930), John F. Kennedy's eminent adviser McGeorge Bundy (1919-1996), and politician John Kerry (born 1943) were all Skull and Bones members, known as "bonesmen". Despite its members' fame and fortune, little is known about the society itself, though it would seem that it plays an important role in decision-making circles of the political, economic and media worlds.

George Bush struggled with alcoholism until the age of 40 and managed to overcome his addiction through rediscovering his Christian faith and the Evangelist church when he became a Born Again Christian.

Though Bush was born in New Haven, Connecticut, Bush's allegiances lie instead with Texas. He bought the local Texas baseball team the Rangers in 1989 with several friends before becoming Texas state governor in 1995 in an election against the popular democrat candidate Ann Richards (1933-2006). He was re-elected in 1998 with 69% of the vote.

In 2000, he won the US presidential election against democrat Al Gore, following in his father's footsteps. He made frequent references to his father, seeking to learn from his mistakes and improve on his successes. The 9/11 attacks which took place not long after his inauguration markedly shaped his presidency and policies, most notably with regards to the Iraq War and the international war on terror. He was re-elected in 2004 against Senator John Kerry (born 1943), and by the end of his second term had only 33% of public support behind him; this was one of the lowest scores of any modern-era president.

At the end of his second term in 2008, Bush retired to his ranch in Texas to dedicate himself to painting. He wrote his own memoirs, published under the name *Decision Points* in 2010, in which he admits to having allowed the CIA to torture Khalid Sheikh Mohammed.

OSAMA BIN LADEN, SAUDI-ARABIAN JIHADIST

Born in Riyadh to a rich Saudi-Arabian family, Osama bin Laden was the spiritual leader of the extremist network known as al-Qaeda. Between 1974 and 1978, he studied commerce and technology at King Abdulaziz University in Jeddah and became part of the family business which specialised in public construction in the 1960s. It was at this time that he began studying the main texts of Wahhabism.

WAHHABISM

Founded in Saudi Arabia in the 18th century by Muhammad ibn Abd al-Wahhab (1703-1792), Wahhabism is a political and religious movement with roots in Islam. It advocates a literal reading of the Quran and condemns all other interpretations as heretical.

He then fought in the war against the USSR in Afghanistan, in which Prince Turki al-Faisal (born 1945) entrusted him with the difficult task of organising transportation to Afghanistan for Saudi volunteers. The young bin Laden therefore became responsible for the fighters' military and ideological training, after which he would educate the widows and children of fallen soldiers. He gradually rose through the ranks, building up an impressive network of contacts and becoming an important figure of Jihadism until Soviet troops withdrew in 1989. In Afghanistan, however, his organisation was far from the only one of its kind. Furthermore, some of the population were suspicious of these radical Saudi troops present in their country. One person who held this opinion was Commander Massoud, who refused to form any alliance with Osama bin Laden.

The young bin Laden received a hero's welcome on his return to Saudi Arabia. Over time, he became more and more critical of the Saudi royal family, especially during the Gulf War (1990-1991), when Saudi royalty opened its doors to American troops. In May 1991, bin Laden decided to leave Saudi Arabia and left on business for Khartoum, Sudan, where he stayed between 1992 and 1996. In 1994, his network of allies in Saudi Arabia, still close to the royal family, disowned him and cut all ties. It was also at this time that he was stripped of his Saudi citizenship.

Between 1996 and 1998, Osama bin Laden called on the Muslim community to attack American interests all over the world. He then became an official enemy of the USA, and was exiled from Sudan before taking refuge in Afghanistan, which had been under Taliban rule since 1996. The US held bin Laden responsible for the attacks on the American embassies in Nairobi, Kenya and Dar es-Salaam, Tanzania in August 1998. In light of this, an international warrant for his arrest was issued first by the Libyan government, and then by Spain and America; a reward of $5 million was offered.

After 9/11, the hunt for Osama bin Laden greatly intensified. He managed to evade capture for many years, every now and then releasing videos in which he threatened the West.

On 2 May 2011, bin Laden was finally found and killed by an American commando in his safe house in Abbottabad, Pakistan. Four other people were reportedly killed during the face-off. His body was then dumped in the sea by American special forces to eliminate its potential of becoming cult figure.

KHALID SHEIKH MOHAMMED, AL-QAEDA MILITARY LEADER

Little is known about al-Qaeda's head of external military operation's childhood and youth. It is thought that Khalid Sheikh Mohammed was born in Kuwait or Pakistan and earned a mechanical engineering degree from a university in North Carolina. He then fought Soviet troops in Pakistan and Afghanistan until 1992.

He was the principal architect of the 1993 attack on the World Trade Center, helped by his nephew Ramzi Youssef. Three years later, Sheikh Mohammed met Osama bin Laden and became part of al-Qaeda. He was arrested on 28 February 2003 in Rawalpindi, Pakistan through a cooperation between the CIA and Pakistani police. He admitted to planning 9/11 and various other missions against the USA when interrogated and tortured. Nowadays however, this information is discredited due to the methods used to obtain it.

He then became one of the CIA's "ghost prisoners", i.e. a prisoner detained anonymously in secret prisons outside American territory. Sheikh Mohammed was subsequently transferred to Guantanamo Bay in 2006 where he was tried before being transferred to mainland America where he awaits further trial.

THE 9/11 ATTACKS

THE TWIN TOWERS

THE WORLD TRADE CENTER

Officially opened on 4 April 1973, the World Trade Center is a complex made up of seven buildings dedicated to business and trade in South Manhattan. It was the work of architect Minoru Yamasaki (1912-1986), and featured two identical buildings known as the Twin Towers. They had 110 storeys each and quickly became a symbol of New York City. After 9/11, the WTC site became known as Ground Zero, and today is home to a museum, a memorial and five new buildings.

On Tuesday 11 September 2001 at 7:59am, American Airlines Flight 11 (AA11) took off for Los Angeles from Logan Airport, Boston. 81 passengers and 11 crew members were on board, having no reason to believe that just 15 minutes later, five terrorists led by the attacks' coordinator Mohammed Atta (1968-2011) would hijack the Boeing 767 and hurtle it towards the North Tower of the World Trade Centre at a speed of 713 km/h. According to investigations, the hijackers reportedly used tear gas to keep passengers away and maintain a constant state of confusion and panic.

The hijackers disconnected the transponder at 8:21am, at which time Boston airport realised what was going on and contacted the Northeast Air Defense Sector (NEADS) at 8:38am, who released two fighter planes to locate and take down the plane less than ten minutes later. But it was already too late; the minute the fighter jets took off, the plane crashed into the first World Trade Center tower.

Witnesses first understood the event as an unbelievable accident, with the plane crashing into five floors of the tower (93rd to 97th). The professional services firm Marsh & McLellan - whose offices were situated on these floors - lost 297 employees on impact. The bank Cantor Fitzgerald, with offices between floor 101 and floor 105, lost 660.

At 8:14am, United Airlines flight 175 (UA175) also took off from Boston heading for Los Angeles, taking 56 passengers and 9 crew members. Half an hour into the flight, five hijackers took control of the plane by force and slammed the Boeing 747 into the South Tower of the World Trade Center at 9:03am at an estimated speed of 872 km/h. Its wings smashed open on impact, releasing kerosene which created massive balls of fire. Huge fires began breaking out in both towers due to electrical short-circuiting caused by the crash.

The World Trade Center towers during the 11 September attacks.

Journalists began flooding towards the scene to cover the incident and filmed the second impact live. It was then that everyone understood that this was no tragic accident; it was a premeditated attack.

At 9:58am, the South Tower collapsed to everyone's surprise, since the towers had been constructed to withstand impact from a plane flying at full speed and the fire this would cause. At 10:28am, the second skyscraper fell which in turn triggered the collapse of the Marriott World Trade Center, a hotel situated right next to the Twin Towers. Both towers collapsed at almost free-fall speed, something which should only occur when no central carrier structures are in place. While this phenomenon is often explained by flooring coming apart and the cast iron used, the exact reason for the towers' collapse remains unknown and is the subject of much controversy.

The collapse of the Twin Towers.

The windows of all buildings within a 130 m radius of the towers were blown out by the force of the impact and an enormous dust cloud spread over the Manhattan skyline, going as far as Brooklyn on the other side of the East River. Almost 1355 people in 1 WTC and 620 people in 2 WTC were killed on impact. Almost everyone working on the floors below where the impact took place was evacuated before the towers collapsed with the help of the 200 firefighting units deployed.

A fourth building situated nearby known as WT7 which housed offices of the secret services and thousands of reports and records on Wall Street investigations also collapsed at 5:25pm. Despite the fact that the building was not targeted by any plane, the debris projected from the Twin Towers impact triggered a fire in WT7 which caused its collapse.

While many observers have blamed American air defence for being ineffective, since it only learned that a second flight had been hijacked after the first crash, blame should not rest entirely with them. On that very day, an important military exercise disrupted the normal functioning and communications between air defence centres. In fact, NEADS only had four fighter jets at its disposal to defend the entirety of North-eastern American territory that two - two in Massachusetts and two in Virginia.

Bush learned of the news while he was attending a reading class in an elementary school in Florida. His reaction was captured on camera, showing the stunned Bush continuing in the children's lesson for several minutes, unsure of how to react. He then improvised a speech in front of the school's teachers and pupils in the school library. He only got back to the White House at 8:30pm that evening, and addressed citizens from the oval office. It was instead New York City Mayor Rudolph Giuliani (born 1944) who emerged as a national hero that day. He arrived quickly at the scene and effectively organised rescue missions, ordering that South Manhattan be evacuated and closing all bridges which linked the island to the mainland. He would be nicknamed Mayor of America and voted Man of the Year by *Time* magazine due to his quick action and how he managed events in the wake of the tragedy.

THE PENTAGON

At 8:20am, American Airlines flight 77 took off for Los Angeles from Washington-Dulles Airport, Virginia. According to estimates in the official report, the plane was hijacked by 5 men at 8:54am who crashed the Boeing 757 into the Western wing of the Pentagon at 9:37am after performing a 330° turn. The transponder was switched off at 8:56am, at which point American Airlines became aware that yet another plane had been hijacked. The Federal Aviation Administration (FAA) warned the NEADS that flight 77 was missing at 9:34am, once more to no avail.

The attack on the Pentagon

The wing of the Pentagon which the plane crashed into had been reinforced with a Kevlar and steel post covering several weeks before. However, several support pillars were destroyed, resulting in the collapse of the building's upper floors half an hour later with a fire starting soon after. In total, the attack on the Pentagon would claim 189 victims, 58 of which were passengers on the flight.

SHANKSVILLE

United Airlines Flight 93, known ever since the incident as the "passenger revolt", was supposed to fly between Newark, New Jersey and San Francisco, taking off at 8:42am. The terrorists on board were apparently armed with knives and hijacked the control desk, cutting off the transponder around 9:28am.

According to the investigation commission, the passengers had been made aware of the series of attacks on the World Trade Center and, fearing the same fate, mounted a rebellion against the hijackers. It is thought that the passengers themselves voluntarily crashed the plane to ensure that the hijackers could not reach their target. Khalid Sheikh Mohammed admitted under interrogation that the attack was destined for the United States Capitol. The airliner crashed into a field in Shanksville in South Pittsburgh, claiming the lives only of those on board: 33 passengers, 5 stewards, 2 pilots and 4 terrorists.

The exact circumstances of the revolt remain shrouded in mystery, but thanks to phone calls made by the passengers, it is known that one of the passengers, Todd Beamer (1968-

2001) launched the counter-attack with the battle-cry which has gone down in history - "let's roll".

A HUMANITARIAN DISASTER

The tragedy claimed many lives, and the death toll was as follows:

- 2753 people in the World Trade Center including 343 fire-fighters, 23 NYPD police officers, 37 Port Police officers, 127 passengers, 20 crew members and 10 terrorists.
- 189 people at the Pentagon; 70 civilians, 55 soldiers, 53 passengers, 6 crew members and 5 terrorists.
- 44 people in Shanksville; 33 passengers, 7 crew members and 4 terrorists.

More than a decade on, the tragedy of 9/11 continues to claim victims; many of the rescue team and firefighters deployed that day have developed cancers linked to the toxic substances and fumes inhaled after the attack.

A fireman calls for backup as he searches through the rubble of the World Trade Center, four days after the attack.

Some people were saved that day. Such was the case for Port Authority Police Department Officers Will Jimeno and John McLoughlin and Genelle Guzman-McMillan was miraculously found alive among the North Tower rubble by the rescue team around 20 hours after the towers' collapse. She was the last person discovered alive on the scene. Estimates suggest that almost 90% of the people working in the skyscrapers that day were saved.

In total, eight buildings were partially or completely destroyed during or following the attacks - the Twin Towers, the Marriott World Trade Center, 4 WTC, 5 WTC, 6 WTC, 7 WTC and the St. Nicholas Greek Orthodox church. 48 buildings close to the impact site sustained damages.

The black boxes of the planes which crashed into the towers were never found. Only those of the planes which crashed into the Pentagon and the field in Shanksville were recovered.

IMPACT

A TURNING POINT IN AMERICAN POLITICS

While the entire country appeared paralysed in the first hours after the attack, US shock was soon replaced by national mourning and a desire to bring the perpetrators to justice. From that moment, President Bush presented himself as the head of state of a devastated country, whose role it was to guide this thirst for retribution.

While the first months of the Bush administration had been difficult for the President not only due to the controversy surrounding his election but also to Congress being largely critical of him, 9/11 dramatically changed the situation. From then on, the President placed greater emphasis on foreign policy in his rhetoric and the balance of his administration underwent a radical transformation. The influence of the moderate members of the Bush administration such as Colin Powell (born 1937) and Condoleezza Rice (born 1954) decreased rapidly in favour of the nationalist neo-conservative vice president Dick Cheney and Secretary of Defense Donald Rumsfeld (born 1932).

The idea soon emerged that after such a tragedy, the USA had to reaffirm its position as the leader of the free world and defend national security at all costs, as much within US borders as outside them, through preventative measures. Like all American presidents during national emergencies, Bush saw his popularity rise; this endowed him with the legitimacy of popular support which had been lacking until that time.

THE PATRIOT ACT

This favourable swing in public opinion allowed Bush to elevate the war on terror to the government's utmost priority and thus more easily impose the measures and policies which would facilitate this war effort. Amid fears of new attacks, the unsolved case of the anthrax attacks and the ever-present spectre of terrorism which the Bush administration were quick to scream and shout about, Congress allowed the President all means necessary to further his counter-terrorism plan. It was in these circumstances that the USA Patriot Act was passed and came into force. These laws were aimed at combatting terrorism, and the bill was quickly drafted in a state of emergency. Only 66 congressmen and one senator voted against the bill.

George W. Bush signing the Patriot Act.

The Patriot Act gave public authorities the right to spy on the private life of anyone they deemed as suspect through telephone hacking and surveillance of bank accounts and private mail, without any prior legal authorisation and without warning the person concerned. The bill tramples over the principle of *habeus corpus* - a rule which states that no person can be imprisoned without a fair trial - for any non-US nationals, giving the authorities the right to detain anyone they deem suspect without trial for up to one year. The respect for individual privacy, once so cherished by the United States, was no more in the wake of 9/11.

In the continued hunt for terror suspects, the Bush administration created military tribunals which could sentence enemy fighters to death irrespective of American law. While Rice and Powell opposed this aspect of the act, the neo-conservatives once again emerged victorious from the debate. This was topped off by documents known as the Torture Memos - letters sent in 2002 and 2003 by the Deputy Assistant Attorney General which authorised torture in the Guantanamo Bay detention centre. In any case, the veil of mystery covering Guantanamo detainees' living conditions along with the centre's intensive use of waterboarding (a form of torture which simulates drowning) quickly became the subject of strong criticism. At the same time, the CIA increased the number of kidnapped suspects in America and beyond.

AFGHANISTAN AND THE HUNT FOR BIN LADEN

The day after 9/11, an investigated named "Penttbom" (Pentagon/Twin Towers Bombing Investigation) was entrusted to the FBI. Three days after the events, 7000 FBI personnel presented a list naming the 19 hijackers with the help of other countries' intelligence services. Two of those listed were from the United Arab Emirates, one was Libyan, one Egyptian and the others were all Saudi-Arabian. In light of the attack perpetrated against Commander Massoud two days before 9/11 and the 1993 World Trade Center attacks, the authorities rapidly turned their attention towards al-Qaeda and its leader Osama bin Laden, who was reportedly hiding in the Afghan mountains.

On 14 September 2001, the USA openly declared that bin Laden was responsible for the attacks and dedicated all necessary resources to capturing him dead or alive. However, it was not until 13 December 2001, that bin Laden would release a video claiming responsibility for the attacks. While terrorism had always been associated with individuals acting alone, this time things seemed different. In October 2001, the USA decided to broaden its counter-terrorism offensive to include an outright attack on Afghanistan, with the ruling Taliban refusing to hand over bin Laden. This war, which came to an end in 2014, would not in fact facilitate the capture of the al-Qaeda leader nor would it dismantle his network, though Taliban operations were stalled.

Barack Obama and his team oversee the raid, led by members of the SEAL, from a distance.

Bin Laden was finally killed on 2 May 2011 in Pakistan. The search had taken a full decade, eventually coming to an end in a fortified complex on the outskirts of Abbottabad where bin Laden was living. He was killed during a raid conducted by 20 members of the SEAL (the US Navy's primary special operations force), and his body was identified in an American military base in Afghanistan. His remains were then dumped in the sea.

CONSPIRACY THEORIES

After the emotions of the tragedy had cooled, concerns regarding the irregularities in the official version of events were quickly raised. Numerous organisations such as ReOpen 911 or the 9/11 Truth Movement made strong claims that 9/11 was a conspiracy orchestrated by the American government, or that the government was at least aware of al-Qaeda's plans. Even in the present day it is difficult to separate what is really true from what is claimed to be true among the many theories which have been proposed with regards to the tragedy. Certain points merit proper discussion and are explored below:

- 7 WTC's collapse: the official version of events from the National Institute of Standards and Technology (NIST) asserts that 7 WTC collapsed due to a fire and seven internal columns being destroyed. However, independent investigators claim that these elements would not be sufficient to cause the building to collapse entirely. Furthermore, the building fell at free-fall rate which has led many theories to point to the idea that this was instead a controlled demolition.
- The collapse of 1 WTC and 2 WTC: some researchers have also proposed theories that a controlled demolition took place in 1 and 2 WTC. This has been largely supported by the fact that many witnesses claim to have heard sounds of explosions just before the towers collapsed. Furthermore, thermate residue (a substance used in controlled demolitions) was found among the debris.
- The way in which Larry Silverstein, owner of the World Trade Center lease, behaved. This American millionaire signed a 99-year lease on the WTC complex on 24 July 2001. In addition to the fact that the complex did not bring in any money, it was also built with asbestos, a toxic material which is extremely costly to remove. As such, Silverstein took out an insurance policy on the complex.

After 9/11, he requested to review his rights under the policy, and found out he was to receive $4.6 million in damages. More troubling still is the fact that the businessman generally held meetings in the restaurant in one of the Twin Towers; that particular morning, he cancelled the meeting for a doctor's appointment and his two sons, who also worked in the complex, arrived late.

- The Pentagon: very few images of the attack on the Pentagon exist. Investigators have therefore proposed that the American Army accidentally fired a missile into the building in an attempt to destroy the plane, meaning that it was not in fact a terrorist attack at all.
- The disappearance of flight 93: very little debris was found in Shanksville from the 100-tonne plane which was supposed to have crashed there. The official version of events holds that the Boeing aircraft crashed into the ground making a crater which closed on itself. Some investigators have also advanced a theory that a missile was used in this case. Furthermore, debris was found scattered 13 km from the site of impact.
- The telephone calls made by the crew: the limits of mobile phone networks in 2001 would not have allowed passengers to make calls while travelling at the speed and altitude mentioned in the official FBI reports. Furthermore, one phone-line stayed connected for 45 minutes after the plane was supposed to have disintegrated completely.
- Videos of hijackers: no images at all have been released of the hijackers boarding the planes despite the fact that airports are littered with security cameras.

SUMMARY

1993
26th Feb.: First attack on the World Trade Center

2001
11th Sept.:
7:59am: Flight AA11 takes off
8:14am: Flight UA175 takes off
8:20am: Flight AA77 takes off
8:21am: Flight AA11's transponder is disconnected
8:42am: Flight 93 takes off
8:46am: Flight AA11 crashes into the World Trade Center North Tower
8:54am: Flight AA77 is turned around
9:03am: Flight UA175 crashes into the World Trade Center's second tower
9:37am: Flight AA77 crashes into the Pentagon
9:58am: The South Tower collapses
10:03am: Flight 93 crashes into a field in Shanksville
10:28am: The North Tower collapses

- On Tuesday 11 September 2001, three airliners are hijacked. Two of them crash into the Twin Towers, buildings which were symbols of American capitalism and power while the third targets the Pentagon, the headquarters of US Department of Defense.
- At the same time, a fourth Boeing aircraft, also hijacked,

- crashes into a field in Shanksville, Pennsylvania.
- At 9:58am and at 10:28am, the Twin Towers collapse.
- The death toll on the morning after the attacks was considerable - 2976 victims killed plus the 19 terrorists.
- Osama bin Laden - leader of al-Qaeda - does not claim responsibility for the attack until December of the same year.
- The USA order the Taliban to hand over bin Laden, who was then hiding in Afghanistan. The Taliban refuse and Bush declares war on Afghanistan.
- The *Patriot Act*, the Bush administration's set of antiterrorist legislation, is voted on by the House of Representatives on 25 October 2001. From now on, the American government identify the War on Terror both on American soil and elsewhere in the world as its priority.
- On 2 May 2011, a SEAL team find bin Laden in Pakistan and kill him during the operation.
- Today, the site where the Twin Towers once were is now known as Ground Zero and has become a place for contemplation.

We want to hear from you!
Leave a comment on your online library
and share your favourite books on social media!

FIND OUT MORE

BIBLIOGRAPHY

- Architects and Engineers for 9/11 truth. (No date) *Science of 9/11*. [Online]. [Accessed 28 September 2014]. Available from: <http://www.ae911truth.org/>
- Bacharan, N. and Simonnet, D. (2013) *11 septembre : le jour du chaos*. Paris: Pocket.
- Body-Gendrot, S. (2002) *La société américaine après le 11 septembre*. Paris: Presses Sciences-Po.
- Dasquer, G. and Guisnel, J. (2003) *L'effroyable mensonge. Thèses et foutaises sur les attentats du 11 septembre*. Paris: La Découverte.
- Frau-Meigs, D. (2005) *Qui a détourné le 11 septembre ? Journalisme, information et démocratie aux États-Unis*. Brussels: De Boeck.
- Laurent, E. (2005) *La face cachée du 11 septembre*. Paris: Pocket.
- Lits, M. and Tétu, J.F. (2004) *Du 11 septembre à la riposte. Les débuts d'une nouvelle guerre médiatique*. Brussels: De Boeck.
- Melandri, P. (2013) *Histoire des États-Unis. Le déclin ?* Paris: Perrin. Vol. 2.
- Meyssan, T. (2002) *L'effroyable imposture*. Chatou: Carnot.
- Patriots Questions 9/11. (No date) *Military, Intelligence and Government Patriots Question*. [Online]. Accessed 28 September 2014]. Available from: <http://patriotsquestion911.com/>
- Ray Griffin, D. (2007) *11 septembre, la faillite des médias,*

une conspi- ration du silence. Plogastel- Saint-Germain: Demi- lune.
- ReOpen911. (No date) *Site d'information sur le 11 Septembre 2001.* [Online]. [Accessed 28 September 2014]. Available from: <http://www.reopen911.info/>
- Various. (2004) *11 septembre : rapport de la commission d'enquête. Rapport final de la commission nationale sur les attaques terroristes contre les États-Unis.* Sainte Marguerite-sur-Mer: Éditions des Équateurs.

ICONOGRAPHIC SOURCES

- The World Trade Center towers during the September 11th attacks. Royalty-free reproduction image.
- The collapse of the Twin Towers. © Hans Joachim Dudeck.
- The attack on the Pentagon © US Navy.
- A fireman calls for backup as he searches through the rubble of the World Trade Center, four days after the attack. © US Navy.
- Barack Obama and his team oversee the raid, led by members of the SEAL, from a distance. © Pete Souza.

FILMS AND DOCUMENTARIES

- *9/11.* (2002) [Documentary]. James Hanlon, Jules Naudet and Gédéon Naudet. Dir. France: Columbia Broadcasting System.
- *Fahrenheit 9/11.* (2004) [Film]. Michael Moore. Dir. USA: Fellowship Adventure Group.
- *9/11: The Twin Towers.* (2006) [Documentary] Richard

Dale. Dir. UK: Dangerous Films..
- *World Trade Center* (2006) [Film]. Oliver Stone. Dir. USA: Paramount Pictures.
- *United 93*. (2006) [Film]. Paul Greengrass. Dir. France, UK and USA: Universal Pictures.
- *September 11 – The New Pearl Harbour*. (2013) [Documentary]. Massimo Mazzucco. Dir. Italy.

IMPROVE YOUR GENERAL KNOWLEDGE

IN A BLINK OF AN EYE !

www.50minutes.com

www.50minutes.com

ISBN ebook: 9782806279231

ISBN paper: 9782806282910

Legal Deposit: D/2016/12603/290

Cover: © Primento

Digital conception by Primento, the digital partner of publishers.